To Laurence,

From your great piano student... in all seriousness Laurence, it would be impossible for me to tell you how much you mean to me. Perhaps my musical failures will be forgotten as you read these pages....

Blessings!

John
6-14-04

३६

Hey Mom! It's Jesus!

By
Denise Nutt-Beers

Bookman LLC
Publishing & Marketing

© Copyright 2004, Denise Nutt-Beers

All Rights Reserved.

No part of this book may be reproduced, stored in a
retrieval system, or transmitted by any means,
electronic, mechanical, photocopying, recording,
or otherwise, without written permission
from the author.

ISBN: 1-59453-233-8

Acknowledgements

No work is an individual effort. This is particularly true for <u>Hey Mom! It's Jesus!</u>

For this book, I offer my deepest gratitude to the people of Spring Hill and Neapolis United Methodist Churches. Their willingness not only to receive the gospel, but to proclaim it as well, is the true power behind <u>Hey Mom.</u> For all that I might have taught them, they taught me volumes more. For letting me serve you for six Christ-filled years and for sharing Jesus with one another, I thank you all.

For the gifts of creativity and the ability to shape words into coherent sentences, I thank my mother, Lynda Nutt, and her side of the family. For the gift being able to understand contracts and finances, I thank my late father, Dennis Nutt, and his side of the family. To Uncle Ronnie, I often understand and know much more than I acknowledge. I thank you especially for picking up where Daddy left off those many years ago. To Alvin,, thank you for always believing I could do anything.

For ushering me into the corporate world and rescuing me from poverty, I thank Dave Krikac and Linda Young and the people of DCC. Y'all rock! To repay them and on behalf of its president, Gene Kirby, I encourage every reader of <u>Hey Mom</u> to pray for DCC and its mission to make the world a little safer. One day they may be responsible for sending "incident-specific information or potentially life-saving instruction" within your community.

For his constant nagging of me to "work on Jesus", for his willingness to "squinch" up his eyes and see my slightly distorted vision of the world, for his countless hours of proofing and editing and for his business acumen, I thank Preston Crook. Had he not beat me about the head with a two-by-four of words, this book would probably never have come to fruition.

For 20 years of unfailing support, for love beyond measure, for patience when there should have been none, for years of being a "pastor's husband", for riding the roller coaster that is a relationship with me, for being a fabulous dad and for really and truly believing I could (and would) do it, I thank my husband, Jim. Without him, I have no idea where I would be.

And for being the greatest and most precious gifts and proudest accomplishments of my life, I thank my children: Daniel, Maylen and Jackson. They are the reason the days are beautiful and the nights are sweet. Without them, nothing else matters.

Most importantly, I give glory to God. It is only through Christ that this and all things are possible. May God bless each of you in the reading and sharing of these words.

So be it. Amen.

The Scripture quotations contained herein are from the New Revised Standard Version Bible, copyright © 1989 by the Division of Christian Education of the National Council of the Churches of Christ in the U.S.A., and are used by permission. All rights reserved.

Hey Mom! It's Jesus!

Where in the world is the little Baby Jesus? For years, that question was asked each December in a small community deep in the South.

During Advent, the first season of the liturgical year beginning four Sundays before Christmas and ending on Christmas Eve, the members of two rural United Methodist Churches took turns hosting the Baby Jesus. While serving as pastor, I began the "Baby Jesus" ministry on the first Sunday of Advent each year. On that day, I would choose the first family to host the Christ Child for the opening evening of the ministry.

The host family received a small Baby Jesus figurine and a blank journal. They were to keep Baby Jesus in their home for 24 hours, recording their thoughts, feelings and experiences in the journal. By 6:00 p.m. the next evening the host family would choose the next household to receive Baby Jesus. They were then responsible for delivering the figurine and journal to the family of their choice, who would then repeat the process, and so on, until Christmas Eve.

I asked that the receiving family call me each evening to notify me of Baby Jesus' whereabouts. They were also asked to sign the front of the journal to help families see where Jesus had been and decide where he would go next. I encouraged the congregations to include shut-ins and those in nursing homes in the ministry by offering to transport Baby Jesus from place to place if need be.

Choosing the first household to host the Baby Jesus each year always required much prayer and consideration. Some years, the first family may have recently experienced a difficult time. In other years, with God's leading, I would choose someone new to the church community. During the first year, I made the decision for the second year just as Advent came to a close.

On the first Christmas Eve, I shared stories of the Baby Jesus' travels with the congregation. That cold, shivery, holy night, a woman confronted me immediately following the service. "You better think about the *politics* of that Baby Jesus ministry you are doing. Some people kept him *two or three days*. But *I* never got him at all!" she fairly shouted.

Foregoing an opportunity to help her reflect upon the reasons that no one asked her to host the baby, I held the conversation in my heart. The next year I selected her as the first host for the infant Christ. Although she chose not to share her experience in the journal, I trust that her inclusion in the ministry must have meant something to her.

Each year, the circumstances differed, but the ministry remained the same. Folks had a chance that few people receive—an opportunity to care for, reflect upon and enjoy having Jesus in their homes and lives in a new and different way.

On Christmas Eve, whoever "had" Baby Jesus was asked to make sure he attended services that night. It was, after all, his birthday celebration! Each year, Jesus arrived. Sometimes he was in a different "manger" or "swaddling cloths", but he always returned, bearing stories of epiphany, transformation, conversion and hope.

Here are the stories, told in the words of those who wrote them. For those who wished, their names were changed to protect their identity. An "*" will appear by their names the first time they are used. The entries are edited only for punctuation and, in rare cases, clarity. Most entries are signed; others are not. All that was written is included here. It started in…

Hey Mom! It's Jesus!

1995

Denise Nutt-Beers

On the first holy night, he was born in an everyday manger. On a holy night in 1995, he was kept on an everyday entertainment center. No matter how things change, they always remain the same...

And she gave birth to her first born son and wrapped him in bands of cloth, and laid him in a manger, because there was no place for them in the inn.

Luke 2:7

Hey Mom! It's Jesus!

We received Baby Jesus last night at church. He was entertained by the wonderful music of the children's and adult choirs. He was placed with our largest nativity set on the entertainment center along with the baby from this set. He lodged in our house with 12 other Baby Jesus figures; you see we have quite a collection of nativity sets. I feel this is the true meaning of Christmas. This child, you see, started it all. Because of this child, there is hope in our future. So as we prepare to deliver this child to someone else tonight, we are not empty. I truly hope everyone has some reminder in their home of this child and the true meaning of Christmas.

Denise Nutt-Beers

New to the South and to the church, the Leitze family brought a son and two daughters to the brick church on the corner. They are musical, creative, and patient—willing to do whatever is necessary to ensure that the gospel of Jesus Christ is shared with those who suffer and long for salvation. The sustentation that their faith has given them is a powerful witness in a world where it is easier to give up and give in than to stand proud and stay strong.

…just as you did it to one of the least of these who are members of my family, you did it to me.

Matthew 25:40b

Hey Mom! It's Jesus!

Baby Jesus was delivered to us by a kind and loving hand at about 6:00 p.m. We welcomed him with open arms and open hearts. As I carried Baby Jesus around with me, doing my daily routine, I realized that this is the way it always is - Jesus is with us at all times, not just when we go to church, sing carols or decorate for Christmas, but always. We sometimes forget that he is with us, no matter where we are or what we do.

I had to make a trip to Nashville and took Baby Jesus with me. As I looked at him sitting beside me in the car, I couldn't help but smile as my mind pictured a donkey with a child safety seat. Jesus loves the little children – and it is our duty to love them also, so that we can to keep them safe.

I picked Baby Jesus up, and he was very cold. I was surprised. Then I thought about it and realized – of course, he is cold. With so many of his people without food or shelter, he feels what they feel – their cold, their hunger, their pain. We must do what we can to help.

"For I was hungry and you gave me food, I was thirsty and you gave me something to drink, I was a stranger and you welcomed me, I was naked and you gave me clothing, I was sick and you took care of me, I was in prison and you visited me…Truly I tell you, just as you did it to the least of these who are members of my family, you did it to me." (Matthew 25:35&40)

May we all reach out – throughout our life – not just during the holidays – to help and love our brothers and sisters – for we are all one with the Lord.

Travis, the young man writing here, faced incredible adversity. His father died very suddenly when he was four and his mom was in her early 20s. Although grief-stricken, they trusted in God and slowly survived that tragic time. When his mother, Connie, was offered a second chance for love, she gained a wonderful new father for her little boy and went on to have two more children.

Travis, diagnosed with Juvenile Diabetes at age 15, handled his new health regime with grace. Continuing to maintain excellent grades, he was active in many sports as well as the drama team at school. With a beautiful singing voice and God-given charisma, he spent his teenage years as a leader, not only in the youth group, but in the church as well.

Attending Lambuth University on a full scholarship and graduating with a double major, this promising young man answered the call to full-time youth ministry. Now married, he will continue to make a difference in the world. With great things still to come, he wrote the following passage at age 16.

But the Lord said to me, "Do not say I am only a boy; for you shall go to all to whom I send you, and you shall speak whatever I command you. Do not be afraid of them, for I am with you to deliver you, says the Lord."

Jeremiah 1:7-8

Hey Mom! It's Jesus!

Baby Jesus had a busy day today. As I was getting ready for school this morning, I forgot about him. I had planned for him to go to school with me, but in my busy morning, I forgot. I then learned my first thing about Jesus. Many people, during their hectic schedules, neglect Jesus and forget that he is always there. I came back home after I got to school and got Jesus, so he could go with me. When I got back to school, I went to the attendance office and explained to the attendant why I was late. Although she understood, it was still an unexcused tardy. So I learned something else: Using Jesus as an excuse cannot keep you out of trouble. After all of that fun, Baby Jesus took an algebra test with me and then we studied for other exams this week. It was a real experience.

Denise Nutt-Beers

A woman of invincible strength, indelible opinions and incredible faith, Jane, a mother of five grown daughters, recounts going to church as a young woman, with her children walking behind her. Every few years the line would lengthen as another began to walk and another baby was born. In they would walk, Mama in front, the ones who could walk following behind, Daddy bringing up the rear carrying the baby.

The legacy she leaves to the church is her complete commitment to God, the church and it's ministries; five strong, grown children, each of whom is active in church; and the education and edification of multiple generations of families who have been touched by her ministry. She may fuss if someone brings a drink into the sanctuary, but she will be the first one at the house with dinner if she knows someone who is sick.

She girds herself with strength and makes her arms strong. She perceives that her merchandise is profitable. Her lamp does not go out at night. She puts her hands to the distaff, and her hands hold the spindle. She opens her hand to the poor and reaches out her hands to the needy.

Proverbs 31:17-20

Hey Mom! It's Jesus!

This was not the first time Baby Jesus had spent the night in my home. As long as I have been married, there has been a manger scene in my home during the Christmas season. From early childhood, we tried to teach our children the real meaning of Christmas. As one time, we invited an elderly bachelor neighbor to come and spend Christmas Eve night with us. It had been many years since he had been around a Christmas tree on Christmas Eve. We shared our love with him on Christmas morn as five little girls dashed around looking at what Santa brought. He was truly thrilled as they excitedly showed him their gifts. When I received him, Baby Jesus was not placed with my other manger scene, but stayed close by me as I moved from place to place in the house. Many thoughts rushed through my mind during the time he spent with me. How his love brought me through times of grief, gave me hope in times of trouble and helped me make decisions in difficult times.

I like to think of God's love through Jesus Christ being in my home each day, directing my path day by day. I like to think of him as watching over me and taking care of my loved ones and of me. And knowing that he is near causes me to say many times, "thank you for my many blessings."

Denise Nutt-Beers

The Burgess Family is a "pillar" in the church. Active in all levels of ministry, if the doors of the church are open, one of them is bound to be there.

Although Tommy, the husband and father, grew up in church, he had never been baptized. After much discussion and prayer, I was honored to offer this sacrament to him and his family. What a day of celebration that was! He served for several years as the Chair of the Administrative Board (the church's governing body). He led with fairness, strength and honor.

Bonnie, wife and mother, was often my right hand in ministry. Together, she and I and a few other churchwomen completely redecorated the Sunday School rooms in the church. She helped with children's choir, Vacation Bible School, church suppers and anything else asked of her.

The girls, Hannah and Meredith, were adorable little blondes full of themselves, delighting the church with their presence each week. They are now fine young women becoming leaders in the church and community.

…obey Christ, not only while being watched and in order to please them, but as slaves of Christ, doing the will of God from the heart.

Ephesians 6: 5b-6

Hey Mom! It's Jesus!

Some very dear and close friends delivered Baby Jesus to our house on Dec. 17th around 6:40 p.m. My two daughters were so excited!

Earlier in the week, my oldest daughter had already asked, "Whose home was Baby Jesus visiting tonight?" I told her I thought Baby Jesus was at Olivia's house. My husband was totally confused and looked at me quite funny. The girls explained to him what the pastor had announced, and that they hoped Baby Jesus would be visiting soon.

We immediately placed Baby Jesus next to our Christmas tree and lit the candles we placed around him.

As the night progressed, I watched the girls. About every thirty minutes they would run to Baby Jesus, check on him, rearrange his blanket and talk to him.

As adults, we all have special occasions that stick in our memories. I feel certain this night will be one of those special times that our family will remember forever! I hope the girls have learned the true meaning of Christmas, and keep God and Jesus as close to their hearts in their daily activities as they have him tonight.

Thanks to our pastor for a wonderful experience!

Denise Nutt-Beers

Sincere and devoted, the Dexters make sure their children are part, not only of worship, but also of every ministry of the church. When I served the congregation, the children were both young. With brilliant red hair and nonstop smiles, they soon became two of my favorites. The oldest daughter and the quieter of the two, volunteered for any activity in the church. From assisting with communion to starring in Christmas plays, Jessica steadfastly gave her all to everything she did.

Her boisterous younger brother never ceased to bring delight to my heart and a twinkle to my eye. The biblical writer must have had Joe in mind when writing, "and a little child shall lead them." From one Sunday to the next, he regaled us with his questions, comments and views on God. He once made me a crude cross made from two pieces of rough wood nailed together in the center. He was very proud of his offering. He is a strapping young man now, playing football in high school. But to me, he will always be that little boy with an impish grin asking me impossible theological questions, and giving me that splintery wooden cross that is one of my most precious treasures.

The wolf shall live with the lamb, the leopard shall lie down with the kid, the calf and the lion and the fatling together, and a little child shall lead them.

Isaiah 11:6

Hey Mom! It's Jesus!

Having the Baby Jesus in our house brings joy, hope, and peace about that special night. We know Jesus is in our thoughts and our spirits because he is alive in our home. Most Christmas stories, like <u>The Night Before Christmas</u> and so on, were the stories we always read at home; but the night Baby Jesus stayed with us, we read the story of how Jesus was born. We've talked a lot about how Jesus came into this life. How exciting it was to have him in our home. Thanks to our pastor for thinking of a great and wonderful learning experience for my family.

Denise Nutt-Beers

Although constantly on the go between practices, lessons and games, Sue always made sure her two energetic boys were part of the church. Often, she would rush to worship, one or both of the boys in tow, arriving late in an effort I am not sure I would have undertaken had I been in her shoes. Still she was there, armed with prayer requests for those in her life who suffered and celebrated alike.

As typical pre-teen and adolescent boys, the church helped Chris and Geoff grow through sports achievements and injuries, academic struggles and successes, driver's licenses and graduations. Now two fine young men, they stand as reminders that sacrifice and commitment for the sake of one's children is the best gift we can offer to God.

...and regard the patience of our Lord as salvation.

2 Peter 3:15a

Hey Mom! It's Jesus!

A few weeks ago, I read If Jesus Came to Our House to Christopher and Geoffrey. It was a sweet little book that gave me much to think about. Little did we know that the Baby Jesus would come to visit so soon.

At first it seemed so awesome to have the Christ Child in our home. He is made of china, so we had to be very careful with him. Imagine how awful it would be to "break" the Baby Jesus. He came in a Ziploc® bag. If you think about it, that was much like he came into the world many years ago. The stable was on ordinary stable just as this container was an "everyday" Ziploc® bag. I do think I will find him a box, since I do not want him to have an accident. That's the mother in me.

As usual, we have been very busy, and the Baby Jesus came at a very hectic time. I must confess that we have kept him much too long, two days and three nights. But, the Baby Jesus has been so patient waiting for us to make time for him, to share the story of the nativity from a favorite book. It makes me realize an important lesson. Jesus is always patient as he waits for us to acknowledge him and to make time to be with him. All we have to do is look around, and he is always there. And even if it has been quite some time since we took a few moments to talk with him, he is ready and waiting to help in so many ways.

Today I will take the Baby to visit another family. It is so difficult to let him go, but I realize that if we are to truly have him in our lives, we must share him with others.

We put our nativity scenes out at Christmas but now, I think I will leave one out all year to remind me that he is always here. If I spent more time with him, perhaps my problems would be less important. Merry Christmas!

Denise Nutt-Beers

Dan* and Sandy* Davidson* brought with them to church their adorable children, Leslie* and Terry*. Committed not only to her children, but also to the children of the church, Sandy served as Sunday School teacher to the smallest of the congregation. Beloved by all, she taught the children with stories, crafts and play. Quiet and well-behaved, Leslie and Terry added much joy to the church. As an accomplished seamstress, Sandy helped with Christmas plays and was active in a great many ministries within the congregation.

So they went with haste and found Mary and Joseph and the child lying in the manger.

Luke 2:16

Hey Mom! It's Jesus!

We had Baby Jesus on a cold day at our home. Terry wanted to know where his Mommy and Daddy were. He didn't think a baby should be away from them, so he put him in our Nativity set. We were fortunate to have two figures of the Baby Jesus in one night.

We felt happiness, love and the spirit of what Jesus and Christmas mean to us.

He is in our hearts and minds always. Now, as a Baby he came for a visit with us. We know he is with us now and forever.

We love you, Jesus.

Denise Nutt-Beers

If we were all like Mrs. Quirk, the world would find itself at peace. She is a gentle lady of the finest character. She resolutely fills the pew second from the front every Sunday. She and her late husband, Mr. Jesse Quirk, were pillars in the congregation as long as anyone can remember. In his later years, Mr. Quirk developed Alzheimer's disease. Mrs. Quirk cared for him at home as long as possible. When he moved to a nursing home out of medical necessity, she and their loving children visited every day.

On the rare occasions that Mrs. Quirk missed church, I received a call the day before or the afternoon following services. She always wanted to make sure that I did not think she was out for no reason.

I love her dearly and will cherish each and every memory of her faithfulness, support and teaching.

...even to your old age I am he, even when you turn gray I will carry you. I have made, and I will bear; I will carry and will save.

Isaiah 46:4

Hey Mom! It's Jesus!

It has been a wonderful feeling having this symbol of the Baby Jesus in our home for these two nights. It really makes me think, "What if Jesus should come in person," to be with us for a time. Even though he is always with us in spirit, we can always depend on him. We need only trust and obey him.

Elma Lee Quirk

Denise Nutt-Beers

Gloria and Leroy are Mrs. Quirk's daughter and son-in-law. She began living with them when Mr. Quirk went into the nursing home. Gloria and Leroy walked through many valleys in the days I served the church. Gloria survives a lifelong battle with migraines, and Leroy is a cancer survivor. They faced the illness and death of Gloria's father, the cancer and death of Gloria's brother and the death of a precious nephew. Through it all, they placed their trust in the Lord. I know that at times their burdens were almost unbearably heavy, yet their faith remained unshakable.

Their sons and daughters-in-law carry the same gentleness and faith into yet another generation. Successful and accomplished, Eric and Phil remind us all of the benefits of being raised in a loving, Christian home. I am honored to know them.

Even though I walk through the darkest valley, I fear no evil; for you are with me; your rod and your staff – they comfort me.

Psalms 23:4

Hey Mom! It's Jesus!

I have certainly enjoyed having Baby Jesus in our home overnight. I feel blessed to have him in our lives. I often wonder how people get through some of life's situations without the Lord to strengthen them. I feel that I sometimes get caught up in such a frenzy of so many things happening at once that having Baby Jesus at home with us has made us more mindful of the need to slow down and take our time. I took Baby Jesus to work with me this morning and shared him with others I work with, explaining what I was doing with him at work. I had a more peaceful day at work with him on my desk beside me. I appreciate having had him visit with us.

Leroy and Gloria Ann Burns

A wonderful night, this! Watching the kids incorporate this baby into their little lives as easily as if he were "real" brought to mind the command of Jesus, which told us that to enter the kingdom of heaven, one must become as a little child. Innocent. Open. Loving. Trusting. Pure.

As unintentional witnesses and tellers of the gospel story, my children enacted the Great Commission as if they were seasoned missionaries. They received Jesus straight into their hearts. They placed him in the center of their lives. They told his story to people who had not heard. They shared him to those who did not have him.

What else is there ever to do?

Go therefore and make disciples of all nations, baptizing them in the name of the Father, and of the Son and of the Holy Spirit, and teaching them to obey everything that I have commanded you. And remember, I am with you always, to the end of the age.

Matthew 28:19-20

Hey Mom! It's Jesus!

How excited we were to receive the Baby Jesus on Daniel's birthday! It was such a special surprise to have Jesus at our party. We decided to put him in the center of the table, and when Daniel opened his presents, the baby sat on top of the couch and watched. Maylen tried to take his blanket off and had to be continually reminded to leave him covered. Jackson said, "Jesus," several times.

We had some company who were not aware of our project. When we asked Daniel if he wanted Jesus to watch the present opening, there was a pause and then the question, "WHO?" When the intent of the project was explained, our friends were intrigued and interested in what we were doing.

Perri Lynn spent the night with us last night. As our guest, we let her keep Jesus beside her bed for the night.

The best part of hosting Jesus, however, was that he kept our focus on him. It did not seem abnormal or unusual to have him, however, because he is such a large part of our lives. It was more like, "Hey everyone, here's Jesus! Scoot over and let him sit down." Like our close friends that celebrated Daniel's birthday, Jesus was a friend, a loved one, and part of the family who stopped in to spend a special night with us.

I knew immediately that I could count on Jesus to add light and life to our evening and our lives just as he came into our world to bring light and love.

A quote from Daniel about his experience with Baby Jesus, "I thought it was great. I love him."

Many Blessings!
The Beers/Nutt-Beers Family

Denise Nutt-Beers

A farmer and a teacher, Sam and Frances Smith embody small town, country life. Living in a house made by their own hands on land populated with hand-raised cattle and an ever-increasing population of antique tractors, Sam and Frances raised three extraordinary children. They now teach another generation the value of hard work, honor and strong family values.

Sam and Frances have been part of our lives since the late 1950's when they and Jim attended school together. While Sam and I agree on virtually nothing politically, I do make him listen and he does make me laugh. He and Frances are the first to respond with help for everything from flat tires, broken water mains and missing stair rails to donations for youth camp, church leadership and constant support.

Frances did not have a chance to write an entry in the journal when she hosted Baby Jesus. She wrote, "Please save this page for us," and sent Baby Jesus on his way. A few days later, she gave me a piece of paper torn from a spiral notebook. These are the words she wrote.

Who is wise and understanding among you? Show by your good life that your works are done with gentleness born of wisdom.

James 3:13

Hey Mom! It's Jesus!

"Please save this page for us."

On a separate page:

The Baby Jesus arrived at our house Saturday about 3:00. The timing was perfect. We had just finished a day of weaning and separating calves and cows and were starting to prepare for a family reunion on Sunday. Who better than the Christ Child to be at a Christmas family reunion!?

Even though Jesus is always an important and ever-present part of our family and home – having the infant Jesus was different. It's been a long time since we've had a baby to care for. It seemed strange for us to be caring for Jesus when we've been so used to having him care for us and be our strength.

It was such fun showing him off to friends and family, carrying him to church Sunday morning and to open house at the parsonage Sunday evening. It was touching to see how other families cared for him with swaddling clothes and a more protective carrying case, making him a part of everyday family life.

Thank you, Denise, and thank you, Baby Jesus, for such a warm and special Christmas experience.

Sam and Frances Smith and family

Denise Nutt-Beers

Sue and Fred entered our lives right on the end of the very front pew. There they started; there they stayed. Wonderfully gifted thinkers and writers, Sue and Fred often provided to me a haven of empathy and stimulating conversation. Wry senses of humor and curiosity allowed Sue and Fred to grow and explore in faith and knowledge.

Fred also allowed me to share a rare moment of spiritual conversion. In his 60s, Fred made the decision to become part of the body of Christ through the sacrament of baptism. Early one evening, the water dripping from my hands mixed with the tears overflowing from my eyes, Fred knelt in a small wooden sanctuary with Sue by his side. When he arose, a baptized child of God, I am positive that I heard a great and wondrous shout from heaven.

The Lord, your God, is in your midst, a warrior who gives victory; he will rejoice over you with gladness, he will renew you in his love; he will exult over you with loud singing as on a day of festival.

Zephaniah 3:17-18a

Hey Mom! It's Jesus!

We received the Baby Jesus as a small package yesterday.

It causes us to recognize that life comes to us each day in a small package of 24 hours. Some of these packages bring joy and laughter; some of them bring us sorrow.

Many days, we are so engrossed in our day-to-day operations, we never even bother to open or check out the package. We miss out on a lot of things this way.

The small bundle with Jesus should remind us he brings each of these packages to us, and we should acknowledge and appreciate each of them. They are our life, and he is part of our life everyday.

Happy birthday Jesus!

Sue and Fred

Denise Nutt-Beers

Emily and Joe Butler, a charming couple, live in the country near the church. Quiet and unassuming, their lives are ordered and accomplished. Joe is a talented farmer, Emily a homemaker and cook. Emily and Joe are the sort of folks that are rich in resourcefulness, wealthy in ingenuity and gifted in all things simple. I never saw them rush, lose their temper, act unkindly or show signs of modern-day stress. They are who I will always wish to be.

And Emily can make the best fried peach pie in the South!

Therefore, my beloved, be steadfast, immovable, always excelling in the work of the Lord, because you know that in the Lord your labor is not in vain.

I Corinthians 15:58

Hey Mom! It's Jesus!

We got Baby Jesus at the Christmas program on Tuesday evening. We brought him home, and Emily put him in a manger beside our bed. It made us think about what Jesus is all about. He's a person who is present in our everyday life. He reminds us to be kind, giving, helpful, sharing, and above all to love others, family, friends and country.

Joe B.

When we went to bed, I told Joe, "Be sure not to snore tonight," but he did. I am so glad that Jesus is good at forgiving. I wish I were better at that. Today is a very busy day, cleaning house and preparing to have my sister and brother for dinner. I need Jesus' power, strength, and faith to get through these extra chores. Happy Birthday Jesus, and come to see us again.

Emily

Denise Nutt-Beers

One of the nicest women in the congregation, Betty is sister to Joe Butler. The blessing of her experience with Baby Jesus is that she received him, realized and thanked him for the good things in her personal life, and then reached out in prayer for the sick and those outside of her community and country. What a blessing for all!

For truly I tell you, if you have faith the size of a mustard seed, you will say to this mountain, 'Move from here to there,' and it will move; and nothing will be impossible for you.

Matthew 17:20

Hey Mom! It's Jesus!

Baby Jesus was brought into our home on Thursday morning about 8:00 a.m. as I was cooking breakfast. I was glad to receive him. Then I began to remember how Jesus came into my life in June of 1950, and how he has made my health come a long way. There isn't a day that goes by that I don't think of how fortunate I've been to be blessed with good health, a good home, and a good husband. I think of the older people and the sick that need you, Jesus. Look over all of our soldiers – the men and women who are in Bosnia, our peacekeeping mission. Jesus, may all of your people have a wonderful Christmas. We all should think of you, Jesus, at Christmas, now, and through the New Year in 1996.

Bless everyone,

Betty

Denise Nutt-Beers

Hey Mom! It's Jesus!

1996

Denise Nutt-Beers

What a day this was! Losing Jesus when one is the preacher does not speak well for one's calling and vocation. Little did I know that God was trying, once again, to teach me a very important lesson.

Indeed, even though there may be so-called gods in heaven or on earth – as in fact there are many gods and many lords – yet for us there is one God, the Father, from whom are all things and for whom we exist, and one Lord, Jesus Christ, through whom are all things and through whom we exist.

I Corinthians 8:5-6

Hey Mom! It's Jesus!

They say confession is good for the soul. Well, the entire year I have kept up with both Baby Jesus figurines – one for Neapolis and one for Spring Hill. At least I thought I had kept up with them. But on the day I was to begin the Baby Jesus Christmas ministry, I could only find one baby! An extensive search turned up nothing.

Of course, the sermon I preached Sunday morning about the Christ-child becoming lost amid the frantic holiday activities and Christmas glitter didn't help one little bit.

What was I going to do?

Oh yes, I have several Baby Jesus figures in my home: one from a nativity from Jim's mother; one from a nativity handmade in Peru and given to me by a friend at Daniel's baby shower; one from a nativity from Mexico; one from a nativity in which all of the characters are Native American; and one from a nativity my mother brought to me from the Holy Land (not to mention the 12 or so babies permanently attached to their nativity scenes).

The baby from the Holy Land is the one I chose to share. After all, he already is a world traveler. And yes, I know there is a risk that he will be broken, damaged or lost. But isn't there always a risk involved when we share Christ? Like I said in my sermon, sometimes we are so busy looking for Jesus in one certain way that we miss him standing right in front of us. Two days of searching it took me to remember that my house is full of Baby Jesus.

May he fill your home as well.

Denise

We do not know much about Jesus' childhood and adolescence, beyond this one trip to Jerusalem at age 12. It is an odd omission by our modern standards of "reality TV" gone mad. It is obvious from Mary and Joseph's response to Jesus' absence that they were "normal" parents who cared for and worried about this, their first-born son.

Now every year his parents went to Jerusalem for the festival of the Passover and when he was twelve years old, they went up as usual for the festival. When the festival was ended and they started to return, the boy Jesus stayed behind in Jerusalem, but his parents did not know it...after three days they found him in the temple.

Luke 2:41-43, 46a

Hey Mom! It's Jesus!

How fitting that Baby Jesus came to us on the day we celebrate the birth of our baby Keisha. Also, our baby is growing up right before our eyes. Do you think Mary and Joseph felt the same way we do? Happy with each new "first', yet saddened that their child would too soon be "on his own?" Rarely do we think about Jesus growing up. We celebrate his birth, with all of our thoughts and feelings surrounding the "sweet little Baby Jesus." We celebrate his death and resurrection as the man who gave his life for us. But, what about the boy? As he grew he needed love from his mother, guidance from his father, and forgiveness in his heart. As we raise our children, we have to teach them that Jesus was once a child, too. He had problems he had to solve, but not without the love, guidance, support and help of his parents.

The Leitzes

Denise Nutt-Beers

Ever committed to the youth of the church, the Scotts were blessed with the Baby Jesus during a retreat weekend. Jesus at a youth retreat? Miracles do happen – boldly and often!

Dawn and Rich along with sons, Max and Andy are every pastor's dream. Put them in charge of a group or project and everything will be done with flawless design. From the painting of dramatic murals to directing the youth to going on mission trips in rural Tennessee, everything they touched shone with the gospel light.

Moreover as for me, far be it from me that I should sin against the Lord by ceasing to pray for you; and I will instruct you in the good and the right way.

I Samuel 12:23

Hey Mom! It's Jesus!

Baby Jesus came to our family over a long, stressful weekend. In fact, he was with me at times I would never have imagined. He stayed with me during our all-night bowling trip, through rehearsals and through the laughter and tears.

But isn't that the way he is anyway? Funny how a small wooden figure can remind you of his presence quicker or more obviously than some of the other ways we feel his presence – like the sunlight coming through the sanctuary onto the faces of young people singing his praises. Or the laughter and hugs from my small children. Or the squeeze of a hand from a loved one.

His presence in our home is, was and will always be the best gift of any Christmas morning.

The Scotts

Denise Nutt-Beers

Meredith singing to the baby like Mary must have done in that cold, dank manger those many years ago...again, as much as things change, they do remain the same.

Sing praises to God, sing praises; sing praises to our King, sing praises.

Psalms 47:6

Hey Mom! It's Jesus!

Baby Jesus arrived at our home on Thursday night. The girls were very excited. I guess the sweetest moment we encountered was when Meredith was sitting in the kitchen with Baby Jesus in hand singing to him, "Away in a Manger." She had no idea that anyone was around, much less listening! It was the sweetest little voice a person could ever hear!

As I sit writing these thoughts on paper and looking at the small wooden figurine, I hope and pray that our children will always keep the true meaning of Christmas within their hearts. I think they will always remember the Christmas with Baby Jesus!

The Burgesses

Denise Nutt-Beers

Some families move into a community and become part of a church. Danny, Beverly and Zach moved into the community and became part of our hearts. Instant friends with all they meet, Beverly and Danny are committed marriage partners and parents. Zach is the center of their world. Where there is one Taylor, there are always three.

Danny and Zach are two more young Christians whom I had the honor of baptizing. What a day that was, to feel the Holy Spirit pour out on this family!

But you will receive power when the Holy Spirit has come upon you; and you will be my witnesses in Jerusalem, in all Judea and all Samaria, and to the ends of the earth.

Acts 1:8

Hey Mom! It's Jesus!

New to the church, I was honored when asked to look after Baby Jesus for the night. It means so much to my family and to me to take part in something so special.

It's hard not having family here during the holidays and everyday, but the church has opened its arms to my family and me to make it easier for us; and we are so grateful.

This little wooden Jesus symbolizes many wonderful things to me and having him in my home for the night has truly made this a Christmas I'll never forget.

The Taylors

Denise Nutt-Beers

Where would the church be without Michael, Kathy, Perri Lynn and Lindsay - the Langleys? Kathy directs the choir; Michael served as church treasurer. Those two titles, however, do little to illustrate the staggering amount of time and energy that this family – including the girls - freely offers to their church and their Lord. Banners, Christmas décor, full communion cups, balanced accounts, successful fish fry plans, solos, prayers – all stand as confirmation of what they offer to God as their very best.

Once I called Michael in tears because of what I believed to be a potentially volatile situation in the church. Before I could get any words through my tears he said, "Don't worry. I'm taking care of it." And he did. Many, many times, I would look to Kathy, who sat literally at my right hand in the chancel. She always knew exactly what I needed – sing another verse, please get me some water, where are the acolytes, who are the people in the back. I never worried with Kathy at my side.

Yet another great theological insight is found in the few sentences below. Do others realize that Jesus is with them every day? The one question begs the next: If not, are we telling them the good news? If not, why not? The words from Kathy have stayed with me, even unto this day. They are, indeed, the gospel.

You yourselves are our letter, written on our hearts, to be known and read by all; and you show that you are a letter of Christ, prepared by us, written not with ink but with the Spirit of the living God, not on tablets of stone but on tablets of human hearts.

II Corinthians 3:2-3

Hey Mom! It's Jesus!

I came home from work to a chorus of two kids saying, "Guess what we got today. Look around, don't you see it? Look over there, don't you see it?" Finally, Perri Lynn couldn't stand it any longer. "We've got Baby Jesus!" She had placed him on the entertainment center with my Christmas village. She said she thought he looked like he had a dress on. It is 2:00 p.m. on Thursday. I'm off work early. The baby is in the car with me going to school to get the girls. I wonder as I pass other cars, "Do they realize that Jesus is in the car with them, too?" Who will we decide to let the baby visit tonight?

Kathy Langley

Denise Nutt-Beers

With beautiful silver hair and dancing eyes, Lucy is the quintessential mother and grandmother. Her lilting Southern accent and ready smile puts everyone immediately at ease. She and her husband, James, own a little piece of paradise in the rolling countryside. While Lucy feels blessed by her family and friends, those who know her understand that her family and friends are the ones who are blessed by her grace.

And now faith, hope, and love abide, these three; and the greatest of these is love.

I Corinthians 13:13

Hey Mom! It's Jesus!

Well, this is the morning after Baby Jesus came to spend the night with James and me. Baby Jesus came to me last night after a very busy and anxious day. We carried James' mother to the hospital, plus baking, cleaning and gift-wrapping. I was very anxious about little Rachel and Thomas both with ear infections and flu. When I went to bed I put Baby Jesus on the table and thought how blessed I am with my wonderful family and friends! This morning, in the quietness, I picked Baby Jesus up and my mind went back to the birth of my children and grandchildren. First our oldest son and his wife gave us three wonderful little girls, through adoption, which we love dearly, then came the birth of little Megan, Lindsey, Rachel, and finally little Thomas. I thought I could never love another as I did the first one, but with each child I loved them all the same, and each one was like the first!. That is the way it is with the love of Jesus. He loves each of us the same, like we were his very first. I hope and pray that my children and grandchildren will always remember the true meaning of Christmas that we all share a beautiful and wonderful gift – Baby Jesus.

Lucy Lochridge

Denise Nutt-Beers

Since she shared Jesus with her children at school, I almost deleted Sue's journal entry from the book. A tremendous gesture of faith, but would she get in trouble? Since no one complained in the ensuing years and the experience was so positive, I decided to leave the entry as it was. Taking a risk for Jesus - would that we all were so brave.

...and it is no longer I who live, but it is Christ who lives in me. And the life I now live in the flesh I live by faith in the Son of God, who loved me, and gave himself for me.

Galatians 2:20

Hey Mom! It's Jesus!

It hardly seems that a year has passed since the Christ Child came to visit. Again he had come at this busy time of year to remind us what the season is really for. And though he stayed for a brief time last year and will only stay a short time again, much of him remains, long after he has gone.

He reminds me that I don't have to be out "amongst them," as Bill refers to my usual after Thanksgiving Christmas shopping spree, to get the true spirit of the season. This year I am relaxing and doing most of my shopping by phone or catalog instead of fighting for a parking space, fighting for a gift, and then fighting for a cashier to check me out so that I can go to another store and fight all over again.

The baby reminds me that he is always there, and I can't ignore him. He waits patiently for me to wind down and think of him each day. And if I will only listen he will help me get by even better with each passing day. This year I think I may leave my nativity set out year-round to help me carry Christ with me everyday. I don't know why I didn't think of that before now.

Now I must send the baby to another warm home in the neighborhood to help others remember the true spirit of Christmas. But before I let him go, I think I will share him with my school children. Some of them are not well acquainted with him and I would like for them to meet him.

Merry Christmas to all!

Sue

Denise Nutt-Beers

The prayer that Joe proposes here may rival any previous offering. Most Decembers, I feel the exact same way.

Rejoice and be glad, for your reward is great in heaven...

Matthew 5:12a

Hey Mom! It's Jesus!

If Baby Jesus is as tired as I am tonight, he probably would like to sleep through all the 25-day hassle to January 2.

He would wake up to see everyone well, healthy and able to go to work and respect the real meaning of "Jesus Christ" the other 340 days.

Joe Butler

Denise Nutt-Beers

During December of this year, Mr. Quirk left this world and entered the kingdom where he was made whole again. Although we were filled with grief, we also rejoiced in his release from the prison of Alzheimer's Disease.

The Lord sets the prisoners free.

Psalms 146:7b

Hey Mom! It's Jesus!

It was a sad day for us when we received the Baby Jesus because our beloved Mr. Quirk had passed away.

Then I got to thinking that Mr. Quirk is with Jesus, and he is in the wonderful kingdom that is full of Jesus' love and goodness.

I could feel the spirit of Jesus' love. I held the baby in my hand, and although it is made of china, it made my hand warm.

The thought of Jesus just brings warmth anyway.

We keep Jesus in our hearts all year round.

Dan, Sandy, Leslie and Terry

We hope everyone has a wonderful holiday and remembers to celebrate the birth of Christ all year long.

Denise Nutt-Beers

The faith passed down through the ministry and teaching of Mr. Quirk is evidenced in the words of his daughter.

Very truly, I tell you, you will weep and mourn, but the world will rejoice; you will have pain, but your pain will turn into joy.

John 16:20

Hey Mom! It's Jesus!

Jesus came to our house yesterday from church after being brought to us from a dear friend.

It is especially comforting to have Baby Jesus visit us at this time since we have just lost our precious Daddy and husband, Jesse Lee Quirk. He (Jesus) has been such a blessing to our family during this long illness and then death. Daddy went to be with Jesus and his Father so peacefully last week; and that very last day Mama and Daddy had had a prayer together, even though Daddy had been barely able to speak. Our faith and the constant love of Jesus and the Father have gotten us through some very anxious times.

I am very happy to have Jesus here with us this week as we continue life in a different phase now. I know he will always be there for us and guides us.

I am so grateful for having had Christian parents who passed their values on to our family, because without this, we would be without hope. We have his love and assurance to carry on through this Christmas season.

May Baby Jesus bless each home he enters and leave there peace, joy, and happiness for the season and for all year through.

Gloria Ann (Quirk) Burns and family

Denise Nutt-Beers

When joy and sorrow fills our hearts with equal strength, it is hard to tell where one ends and the other begins. For the Quirks, the loss of Jesse was sad; yet they were filled with relief. Paradox is not new to the Christian community, nor is it likely to disappear any time soon.

Blessed are those who mourn, for they will be comforted.

Matthew 5:4

Hey Mom! It's Jesus!

It is hard to express my thoughts about how I feel at this time. It simply overwhelms me. Both joy and sorrow fill my whole being.

Jesse is gone but certainly not forgotten. He will always be near me in spirit and loving care. I wouldn't call him back; he was in such pain most of the time. Now I truly believe he is happy up there with his loved ones who have passed on. It is hard to understand how the Baby Jesus, as he grew older could be so forgiving of the way he was mistreated and finally died upon a cross for us all.

Love to all,

Elma Lee Quirk

Denise Nutt-Beers

There is safety and love at the feet of Jesus. What blessing he offers to us, his children.

While I was with them, I protected them in your name that you had given me. I guarded them, and not one of them was lost...

John 17:12a

Hey Mom! It's Jesus!

Keeping Baby Jesus in my room made me feel safe and secure. It made me think about the real birth of the Baby Jesus. Now I know why we give the Baby Jesus around. I think that the more you learn about Jesus, the more you understand about the true meaning of Christmas!

Jessica Dexter

Denise Nutt-Beers

There will be showers of blessings when one is attuned to the Lord.

I will make them and the region around my hill a blessing; and I will send down the showers in their season; there shall be showers of blessing.

Ezekiel 34:26

Hey Mom! It's Jesus!

Baby Jesus spent Sunday night with us laying on the night table by the bed.

When I awaken, I thank him for letting us have another day to live. Also, there is a little Bible my great aunt gave me years ago. Everyday I will touch it and say Jesus has "blessed me for another day."

Baby Jesus, I hope you will bless everyone in the troubled world and bring them unto you.

Have wonderful travels from house to house.

He loves you if you love him.

Betty

Denise Nutt-Beers

Jesus as incentive – so many new ways to view the Christ child beyond merely a baby in swaddling clothes lying in a manger!

May the Lord give strength to his people! May the Lord bless his people with peace!

Psalms 29:11

Hey Mom! It's Jesus!

Baby Jesus came to us in the pouring down rain and left in the bitter cold and snow. However, his presence brought such warmth and comfort, as well as the promise of better things. Hosting Baby Jesus helps us to put things in perspective to better realize the real meaning of Christmas. Seeing him lying in the manger gives me the incentive to occasionally sit down, relax, and enjoy a little peace and rest, taking time to appreciate family, friends, warmth, good health, beautiful music, cheerful decorations, and the joy of waiting for our first grandbaby – along with so many other blessings.

We have so many things to be grateful for. Thank you, Baby Jesus, for spending time with us, sharing in our celebration, and reminding us that you are the reason for the season!

Frances Smith

Denise Nutt-Beers

Hey Mom! It's Jesus!

1997

Denise Nutt-Beers

Ask anyone in Spring Hill about Miki and the same response will be heard time and time again. Miki is beautiful inside and out. With flowing red hair and dancing eyes, Miki lights up any room she enters. Her daughter, Taegan, follows in her footsteps. Taegan has faced some obstacles in her life, but always with her sweet spirit and her unfailing courage intact. Miki worked with children in the church and continues to do so in her career. She is gifted in her ability to communicate with them, to see the goodness in every situation and to maintain her patience when others would be screaming in frustration. An outstanding mother and friend, Miki demonstrates a standard of excellence to which all can aspire.

...*for the Lord does not see as mortals see; they look on the outward appearance, but the Lord looks on the heart.*

I Samuel 16:7

Hey Mom! It's Jesus!

Sharing Baby Jesus is such a wonderful tradition. Taegan and I were glad when John and Harlan brought Baby Jesus to us. We had a special place for Him to stay, but he didn't stay there long because Taegan wanted him to go everywhere we went.

Baby Jesus went to the table when we had spaghetti, and we said a special prayer of thanks for having him there with us and for him being with us always.

In Jesus' Loving Name,

Miki and Taegan

Denise Nutt-Beers

As Miki is to motherhood, so Buddy is to fatherhood. His support and love of Taegan knows not limits or bounds. One of my first memories of Buddy is of him shaking my hand and not just telling me, but also showing me with his face and eyes, his excitement about Jesus. Buddy's eyes probably tell the world more than he wants them to, but on that day, I literally looked in his eyes and saw the Lord. Buddy has a tall and commanding presence. With him on the Lord's side, victory will always be assured!

...*for whatever is born of God conquers the world. And this is the victory that conquers the world, our faith.*

I John 5:4

Hey Mom! It's Jesus!

Baby Jesus,

To have Baby Jesus in our home is a great reminder to us that his birthday is coming soon. He is with us in our spirit everyday and everywhere we go.

The Baby Jesus figurine is a refreshing reminder that he gives us hope, love and life, not to mention that he is there to forgive us of our sins. All we have to do is ask him. Yes, that is right, that is what he died for. He is there for us to talk to him, and he will carry our burdens for us while we are on this earth. And when we die, he will give us eternal life. We can trust this promise. Believe it.

Baby Jesus is also a reminder that reaches deep in every one of our hearts, touching us so our faith can grow. We all need to pull together and bond so we can serve our Lord the best we can. That's what we are here for. I pray that everyone who touches Baby Jesus this year will be especially blessed from our Lord Jesus Christ. I feel honored to be included in this brotherly love from all. Thanks.

Merry Christmas to all, in Jesus Christ's name.

Buddy

Denise Nutt-Beers

Jane asks some poignant questions as she hosts the Baby Jesus. But then, Jane asks poignant questions any time she talks about God and faith. Sometimes the questions are uncomfortable. Sometimes the questions are tough. One can rest assured, however, anything Jane asks is for the furtherance of the Kingdom of God.

But to all who received him, who believed in his name, he gave power to become children of God, who were born, not of blood or the will of the flesh or of the will of man, but of God.

John 1:12-13

Hey Mom! It's Jesus!

Having Baby Jesus spend the night in my home is a reminder that the spirit of Christ is present here each day.

God sent his son, Jesus, into the world as a baby. The angel appeared to tell Mary that the child to be born would be called holy, the Son of God. For this I give thanks.

God is love. Let us love one another and forget not to show love.

Do I allow God's spirit to come into my life each day? Do I do unto others, as I would have them do unto me?

If Jesus came into the world today would we be ready to receive him, or would we be too busy with material things about us to receive him?

Many people around us are lonely, troubled or burdened with problems in their everyday lives. If we have love in our hearts, we will take time to visit, bring a word of cheer, correspond or in some way show that we care.

God never ceases to care for us and to be with us if we just ask in prayer, believing.

Thanks be to God for Baby Jesus coming to the world.

May the love of God dwell among us during this holy season.

Jane Simmons

Denise Nutt-Beers

When kids began to speak theologically, adults would do well to listen. Sometimes when we think we need to teach them, they turn right around and teach us instead.

And remember, I am with you always, to the end of the age.

Matthew 28:20b

Hey Mom! It's Jesus!

When I found out we had gotten the Baby Jesus, I felt special. I asked my parents if he could sleep in my room, and they said yes. It was neat because I knew he was right there beside me. Hopefully, everyone knows that he is beside them at all times of the day, helping them and watching over them. Happy Birthday Baby Jesus!

Emily Cathey

Merry Christmas

Denise Nutt-Beers

Rebecca reminds everyone that Christmas is a wonderful season and that life is a loving gift.

They shall be mine, says the Lord of hosts, my special possession on the day when I act, and I will spare them as parents spare their children who serve them.

Malachi 3:17

Hey Mom! It's Jesus!

When we got Baby Jesus, I felt pretty special. I felt like Baby Jesus was watching over me the whole time he was there. This is a wonderful tradition. It should remind people that Christmas is a wonderful season. A season filled with love and joy, and peace and happiness. It reminds people that this is the time of Jesus' birth, and we should all celebrate and rejoice the birthday of our king. I hope everyone feels the spirit of Christmas this season.

In Jesus' name,

Rebecca Cathey

Denise Nutt-Beers

Children who independently and instinctively know that they can spend a moment alone with Jesus are a testimony to their parents' love and teaching.

But whenever you pray, go into your room and shut the door and pray to your Father who is in secret; and your Father who sees in secret will reward you.

Matthew 6:6

Hey Mom! It's Jesus!

We had just returned from delivering a birthday gift to a very dear person in our lives. As soon as we entered the door, Tommy told us that Baby Jesus was on his way! The girls were so excited and immediately began making a special place for him.

Baby Jesus arrived, and we welcomed him with open arms. Meredith so carefully placed him where she and Hannah had prepared and gave him a gentle kiss.

We discussed Baby Jesus and what the Christmas season means, and that it was our way of celebrating the birth of our King.

During the night, I witnessed both girls going to Baby Jesus and taking a moment to talk with him quietly. At these times, it seemed to me they were in their own little world with him. I can only pray that they carry the spirit of Christmas throughout their lives and that they will always take time to talk to our Lord.

Our family feels very special to be a part of this tradition each year of sharing a night with Baby Jesus. We hope we can spread that joy by delivering him to another special family.

In Christian love,

The Burgess Family

Merry Christmas to Everyone!!

Denise Nutt-Beers

Jimmy and Melissa and their girls were initially brought to the church by the annual fish fry. Jimmy, a friend of church member, Tommy, who was in charge of purchasing the fish for the church fish fry, owned a catfish restaurant. And the rest is history.

When the Hughes family came to the church it was as if they has always been there. Jimmy and I have been friends since grade school, and it gave me pause to have someone who "knew me when" sit there in church every week. Would he believe me as a pastor? Could he get past the high school antics, the really bad hair of the 1970s, the fact that for most of elementary and junior high, I was taller than he? Could I?

The answer is a resounding yes! One Easter Sunday, I administered the sacrament of baptism to the entire family. When I got to Jimmy, I paused and began to speak to the congregation while he begged me under his breath not to say anything. But what I had to say was this: What a testimony to the work of the Lord in me and in him that God could bring two skinny, goofy fifth graders to the altar to participate in the most holy of acts. How great is the Lord that we could be there, surrounded by our families, and bound by time and history ready to step out in faith for the gospel.

When they had gone ashore, they saw a charcoal fire there with fish on it, and bread. Jesus said to them, "Bring some of the fish you have just caught." Jesus came and took the bread and gave it to them, and did the same with the fish.

John 21:9-10, 13

Hey Mom! It's Jesus!

This is our first year to have Baby Jesus to spend the night with us. We feel very honored and excited to share in this tradition.

First, he sat with Jessica while she finished her homework, and it has been a long time since she made it through homework without crying or being upset.

Then, he watched Whitney and Jessica put ornaments on the family Christmas tree that looks so wonderful. The presence of Baby Jesus makes this special time in our family that much more memorable.

Baby Jesus also helped us to take time out of our busy holiday activities to remember the reason for the season.

Merry Christmas to all!

Jimmy, Melissa, Whitney and Jessica Hughes

Denise Nutt-Beers

Perri Lynn is a theologian, but she has no idea how profoundly she speaks. Head in the clouds, feet planted firmly on earth, Perri Lynn keeps us grounded in what's real.

...but for God all things are possible.

Matthew 19:26

Hey Mom! It's Jesus!

When Baby Jesus spent the night with us it was (I think) the best day of my life, but I had too much homework.

Today was the best day of my life because my boyfriend called me at home, and I think that was all Baby Jesus' doing.

We put Baby Jesus with our nativity set with Mary, Joseph, three Wiseman, three shepherds, two camels, a donkey and a cow. There was another Baby Jesus, so I scooted that one over and made it look like Mary had twins.

Jesus' child always,

Perri Lynn Langley

Denise Nutt-Beers

Lindsay is another child who has grown up and gone away to college. Her faith was remarkable even as a little girl. By God's grace, it has matured with her and stands her in good stead even today.

I will cause your name to be celebrated in all generations; therefore the peoples will praise you forever and ever.

Psalms 45:17

Hey Mom! It's Jesus!

When Baby Jesus came to spend the night at our house, I was excited. I felt Jesus was watching over me every second that he was here. This should remind people that Christmas is a great season. It is a season of loving, caring, and giving. Let us all celebrate the birth of our Baby Jesus in this wonderful season and year. Have a great year of 1998. Merry Christmas to all.

In Jesus' loving name

Lindsay Langley

Denise Nutt-Beers

A spirit of thanksgiving permeates the orange-bricked Taylor home, not only at Christmas, but also through the year.

For this reason I bow my knees before the father, from whom every family in heaven and on earth takes its name.

Ephesians 3:14-15

Hey Mom! It's Jesus!

First I would like to thank the Langley Family for bringing Baby Jesus to our loving home. It is such a great pleasure to have Baby Jesus in our home for a second straight year.

I thank the Lord for bringing us together, and the church for extending their arms and welcoming my family as if it were your own.

By taking Baby Jesus from home to home, it shows us that giving, sharing and loving each other is what the Christmas spirit is all about.

May God bless everybody, and may everyone have a merry, merry Christmas.

The Taylor Family

Denise Nutt-Beers

Barbara and Lee are integral persons in the Spring Hill congregation. With years of wisdom and experience, Lee's presence at meetings always ensures an informative and well-thought-out response to questions. As a physical therapist, he uses his hands to heal in much the same way as Jesus. He has also used the gift of healing in the church community in times of struggle. Ever levelheaded, Lee helps maintain balance and perspective in the often emotion-laden business of the church.

Barbara is always at his side. She, too, offers her wisdom and experience to the church through varying leadership roles. Sundays find her at the organ, playing for the choir and congregation, a smile on her face. She and Lee both have great vision for the future of the church as well as the commitment to bring their vision into fruition.

To the King of the ages, immortal, invisible, the only God, be honor and glory forever and ever. Amen.

I Timothy 1:17

Hey Mom! It's Jesus!

Having Baby Jesus in our home was much different from having a human baby. No crying, no 2 o'clock feedings, etc. He was an addition to our nativity scene and fit in very well. This makes Mary the mother of twins tonight. Tonight we watched a special T.V. show in which Natalie Cole sang this is his birthday. Then she and Wynonna sang a duet, which was very familiar to both Barbara and myself since Travis sang it for our church. The song was "Mary Did You Know".

To have Baby Jesus in our home reminds us that Christmas is for the celebration of his birth. I think we too often lose this idea because of gift buying and partying.

We hope this will be a truly Christian experience for all, and that Christ will be king in our hearts.

Merry Christmas, and may you all be blessed in the coming year.

In Christian love,

Lee and Barbara

Denise Nutt-Beers

Lisa's family moved to Spring Hill with the Saturn Corporation. What a lovely family, welcoming their new pastor into their lives and home! One of Howard's first contributions to the church was a ramp for the side entrance making the church accessible to persons with handicapping conditions. Lisa often worked with the children, organizing several successful Parent's Night Out events. Their two children, Shana and Eric, were delightful additions to the children's and youth groups.

Imagine getting Jesus in church of all places! Shana offers wisdom beyond her years in the words below.

...he was lost and is found! And they began to celebrate.

Luke 15:24b

Hey Mom! It's Jesus!

When we got Baby Jesus, we got him in church. My mom told Eric and me to watch Baby Jesus at church. So when the youth had to rehearse our program, I sat Baby Jesus on the front pew. Then my mom came to bring my medicine and asked where Baby Jesus was. I said "Oh no, hold on, I think I sat him on the pew." So I went and looked, and there he was. I asked my mom to take him home for me. She put him in the manger with the other Baby Jesus. We acted like it was his twin brother. Well, now I guess it is time to pass Baby Jesus on to someone else to enjoy him. Merry Christmas to all.

Shana

Denise Nutt-Beers

Dawn and I connected as working mothers trying to balance home and jobs. The sacrifice is often of the mother's own well-being. Dawn reminds us that God's grace is sufficient, and that only God can be all things to all people.

…but he said to me, "My grace is sufficient for you for power is made perfect in weakness." So, I will boast all the more gladly of my weaknesses, so that the power of Christ may dwell in me.

II Corinthians 12:9

Hey Mom! It's Jesus!

We were given Baby Jesus late Wednesday evening. Rich has been gone all week, the boys have homework, they're hungry and dirty…but Baby Jesus wasn't tired. I sat in the drive-through line at the bank watching other lines going much faster than mine, losing all of my patience…but Baby Jesus doesn't lose his patience with us. I've still got more Star Wars toys and walkie-talkies to buy, and I don't know where I'll find the time…but the gift of our savior's birth is really all we ever need. Isn't it amazing how he can put our lives back in focus?

In Christ,

The Scotts – Dawn, Rich, Max and Andy

Denise Nutt-Beers

Did we ever! Run into problems, that is. In the three entries that follow, the evidence of God's grace is irrefutable! Reaching out to others makes life's problems seem wonderfully insignificant.

...be glad and rejoice, for the Lord has done great things!

Joel 2:21

Hey Mom! It's Jesus!

I was the one who got the call that we were getting Baby Jesus. I was surprised because it was so late I didn't think we would get him. And boy I'm glad we did!. My mom really needed him today (12/22/97). She and Denise ran into some problems. But I am really glad we did get Baby Jesus.

Sincerely,

Jayna Leitze

Merry Christmas

Denise Nutt-Beers

Keisha had some minor surgery during the month of December. It is a testimony to the church and her family that she was fully aware of who was really "in charge" of her recovery and health – Jesus!

They cast out many demons, and anointed with oil many who were sick and cured them.

Mark 6:13

Hey Mom! It's Jesus!

Baby Jesus was born in a manger tonight. He helped me with my segery (sic). He helped me get throw (sic) it.

Keisha Leitze

Denise Nutt-Beers

Once again, Connie skillfully wove together practical reality and perceptive understanding. Michael and Lindsay Langley were working, along with Connie and me, with a family in the community. Taking the money donated for necessities, we went on a shopping spree for food, toiletries, clothing and other essentials. As the sun waned in the sky the day before Christmas Eve, we delivered the bounty to the very appreciative family.

Feeling good about our church and its giving spirit, we laughed and talked as we bustled into our cars after dropping off the supplies, heading home to our own families.

Seconds later, the water for an entire road was knocked out, leaving two pregnant women with no working bathrooms. It was my fault. Entirely.

Then our mouth was filled with laughter, and our tongue with shouts of joy; then it was said among the nations, "The Lord has done great things for us, and we rejoiced."

Psalms 126:2

Hey Mom! It's Jesus!

Baby Jesus came to us today. This is our third year to be blessed in this way. In a way, it saddens me. I can remember very well our first time with the Baby Jesus. Jerry's voice was filled with such joy and enthusiasm as she asked, "Have y'all had Baby Jesus yet?" It made us feel so good that Noel and Jerry thought enough of us to pass Baby Jesus on to us. We felt blessed to know them, that they were part of our lives. They will forever live in our hearts. We thank the Lord every day for the joy they bestowed upon us.

Now, for today. How fitting that he came to us while we were doing his work. It was the day we went to visit a special family…

"The Day That Baby Jesus Came"

by Connie Leitze

The day that Baby Jesus came
Was not an ordinary day.
We all know that what they say is true:
"He works in mysterious ways."

It was a day of jubilation,
The kind that touches your heart.
It was a day of doing the Lord's work,
Of which I was thankful to be a part.

Denise Nutt-Beers

You see, there was this family
Who were experiencing quite and ordeal.
So, the child had written to Santa.
She asked for no toys, just a meal.

The Lord was watching over her.
He made sure our church got her letter.
For he knows his people would go to work
To help make the child's life better.

We went to work on it right away,
Collecting money and presents galore.
It certainly was a sight to behold,
Meeting our expectations – and so much more.

Then our day of fun began,
With Michael, Lindsay, Denise and myself.
We went shopping with joy and love in our hearts,
While we grabbed everything off the shelf.

We raced happily from aisle to aisle,
The joy of giving filling our hearts.
It wasn't long until our buggy was filled.
We had to send Lindsay after more carts!

A Holiday Elmo, on sale nonetheless!
Who can resist such a great buy?
A blanket and hat to keep them warm,
Paper towels and Kleenex® for teary eyes.

Hey Mom! It's Jesus!

Cereal, spaghetti, macaroni and cheese,
And other staples to keep them fed.
Band-Aids® and vitamins to maintain health.
Tylenol® for fever and achy heads.

Anti-bacterial kitchen cleanser and soap,
Dishcloths, dish towels, dishwashing liquid, too.
Bath towels and wash cloths to keep them clean.
Ah, let's not forget the shampoo.

We tried to get everything a family would need
To get by 'till they're back on their feet.
And if we have any money left when we're done,
We can help by paying the bill for their heat

We loaded the van to overflowing it seemed.
We felt like Santa packing his sleigh.
As the joy in our hearts grew stronger each mile,
We thanked the Lord for showing us the way.

We delivered the gifts into grateful hands,
With Baby Jesus at our side.
We said our good-byes with an invite to church,
And I know our smiles had to be two feet wide.

Denise and Lindsay were both driving that day,
Taunting each other about who was better.
But as Denise backed out of that narrow drive,
There was a big thump, and the ground became wetter.

Denise Nutt-Beers

For goodness sakes! What in the world could it be?
A water pipe had jumped in her path!
More and more water came bubbling out of the ground,
But it was really too cold for a bath

Well, we kept calling phone numbers – to no avail.
Seems they all had more important things to do.
Now it looked like a river going out of the drive.
Watch out! Oh, there's mud on my shoe!

Finally a man came to cut off the water.
Why, he was the husband of the little girl's teacher!
Now these poor people had no water at all!
What the Lord giveth is taken away by the preacher!

Well, finally a church member name Sam came along.
Now he is a jack-of-all-trades.
Why, yes, I think I can fix it, he said.
Does anyone here have a spade?

Then a man showed up – no one had called,
A plumbing inspector for the city of Spring Hill.
He helped Sam as he fixed the pipe,
But, how is got there – no one could tell.

I believe that Jesus had a hand in it all,
(Although he had lost his hand in the ordeal).
For the Lord does work mysteriously,
With a Love we cannot conceal.

The Leitze Family

Hey Mom! It's Jesus!

Denise Nutt-Beers

As a third-grade teacher, Sue undoubtedly looks forward to winter break. With the message of Christmas ever in her heart, however, she shared Jesus with her classes. Protecting their privacy by omitting their entries, the students nonetheless reported that Jesus made them feel "even speialer (sic)"; that they love him "like he is"; that Jesus is a "huggable person"; that Jesus makes them feel "confident" and "safe"; and that Jesus is their "best friend". To which I can only add, "Preach!"

Then little children were being brought to him in order that he might lay his hands on them and pray.

Matthew 19:13

Hey Mom! It's Jesus!

It seemed only natural to share the Baby Jesus with my school children. My dear friend, Joe Dexter, brought the baby to me at school this morning. The children wanted to know all about him. I especially enjoyed sharing him with the children who said, "I don't go to church." I invited them to come to our church. Perhaps they will.

It has been a difficult time for me lately with all the many things happening in my day-to-day life at home and at school. I am reminded through this activity that all of these children in my care are just as precious to their parents as the Baby Jesus was to Mary and Joseph and Chris and Geoffrey are to me. They are as precious to their parents as Jesus is to all of us at Neapolis.

Jesus is constant – always there, and he is always the same. That is comforting to know I can count on him always being there no matter how bad things get. And it seems there are so few things you can count on these days.

The holidays have arrived, and I am anxious to get my nativity sets out and enjoy them. I must send this baby on as many others are waiting anxiously for him.

Merry Christmas! And Happy Birthday Baby Jesus!

Sue

Denise Nutt-Beers

Frances had a moment to write when Jesus reached her this year. No matter when she added her entries, she always offered words of inspiration and wisdom.

They answered, "Believe on the Lord Jesus, and you will be saved, you and your household."

Acts 16:31

Hey Mom! It's Jesus!

The one really important thing that having Baby Jesus did for me this year was to make me stop my hectic life for a few moments, to really think about and enjoy the real meaning of Christmas. It was really special sharing him with the entire family – husband, children and grandchildren. Thanks again, Baby Jesus, for making this Christmas a little more special than usual.

Frances Smith and family

P.S. Baby Jesus is going to the Open House at the parsonage tonight. What a special treat for all!

Denise Nutt-Beers

Joe's entries are always two or three sentences long – much like his conversations. What he lacks in verbosity, he makes up for in the weight of the words he speaks.

Now to him who by the power at work within us is able to accomplish abundantly far more than all we can ask or imagine, to him be glory in the church and in Christ Jesus to all generations, forever and ever. Amen.

Ephesians 3:20-21

Hey Mom! It's Jesus!

We got Baby Jesus Sunday afternoon, Christmas is about Jesus and what he has taught the world for almost 2000 years. May this Christmas be for Jesus and his teaching for 2000 years more.

Joe Butler

Denise Nutt-Beers

With the holiday season often comes frenetic activity, even for those of us who are supposed to know "the reason for the season", as the popular phrase goes. Still, we get lost amid ribbons and sales, lights and toys, programs and family gatherings. To pause, even for a moment, to thank the one from whom all things are made, brings us once again to the manger filled with rustling hay and the cooing of a newborn babe.

And the word became flesh and dwelt among us, and we have seen his glory, the glory as of a father's only son, full of grace and truth.

John 1:14

Hey Mom! It's Jesus!

As I finally get a chance to sit with Baby Jesus alone after a busy couple of days it makes me think more of the Birth of Jesus.

We always know he is with us in our busy times and our quiet times.

Dan, Sandy, Leslie and Terry

Denise Nutt-Beers

Mrs. Quirk could write volumes about love. But she doesn't need to do so; in the end...she lives love, which speaks far greater wisdom than any celebrated author could ever compose.

(love)...bears all things, believes all things, hopes all things, endures all things. Love never ends.

I Corinthians 13:7-8a

Hey Mom! It's Jesus!

Today, I have been reading stories in the December issue of Guideposts and these words in one story I have been reading said, "I learned Christmas is not about presents or Santa, but about love, the greatest gift of all. If Christmas isn't in your heart you won't find it under the tree."

How true these words are. Having "Baby Jesus" with us is a wonderful blessing. Let us keep him in our hearts always.

Elma Lee Quirk

Denise Nutt-Beers

The evidence of Mrs. Quirk's love is evident, once again, in the words of her daughter, Gloria, who is a prophet in her own right.

...do not fear, for I am with you, do not be afraid, for I am your God; I will strengthen you, I will help you, I will uphold you with my victorious right hand.

Isaiah 41:10

Hey Mom! It's Jesus!

On Sunday afternoon our family went to visit our son, daughter-in-law and granddaughter in Franklin. We took Baby Jesus with us for the visit. I felt safer on the highway with Baby Jesus in the car with us. It seems to make you concentrate more on the best happening when Jesus is "present" (even through this is a symbol of Jesus in the carved wooden figure). If we just take time to think, he is right there all the time. Our son and family were happy to have Baby Jesus visit. My granddaughter, Hannah, (18 months) took him and carried him around hugging and loving him. This was so touching to all of us. I told her that Baby Jesus loved her too, and she had a wonderful smile.

I feel so blessed that we live in a country where we can participate in activities in our lives such as being free to have Baby Jesus visit with member after member in our congregation and elsewhere.

God bless you everyone as Baby Jesus touches your lives.

Gloria Ann Burns

Denise Nutt-Beers

Hey Mom! It's Jesus!

1998

Denise Nutt-Beers

Dawn's story is one more miracle in the midst of many found along the journeys of Baby Jesus.

And remember, I am with you always, to the end of the age.

Matthew 28:20

Hey Mom! It's Jesus!

I believe that the spirit of Jesus is with us everyday, the good and the bad days. However, there is something magical about the physical presence of "Baby Jesus" in your home.

This year, not only do I know where he was on Sunday and Monday, I know where Jesus was Saturday night. You see, my grandmother was having a heart attack. She was at my aunt's home and had ceased to have a pulse. At the same time, there was a small kitchen fire at the home across the street where firemen and EMT's had been called. Listening to their radio, they heard the 911 call for my grandmother, and the by-standing neighbor informed them it was just across the street and ordered them out of her house to go to my grandmother's aid. Had they not been right there, she would have perished.

Just as the EMT's and the neighbor's heard the call for help, so did Jesus. During the death of my grandfather, I have been praying for him to help heal my grandmother and to protect her.

Isn't it amazing how Jesus' love can be with us, protecting us, even when we aren't aware of it.

"Baby Jesus" moves on now, but his spirit stays with us.

Dawn Scott

Denise Nutt-Beers

Jesus on the entertainment center is a frequent image in these journeys. Found by riversides, on hilltops, around the dinner table, in the dusty streets in Biblical times, today he would likely be found beside entertainment centers, on interstates, in local fast-food restaurants and at the mall.

And I, when I am lifted up from the earth, will draw all people to myself.

John 12:32

Hey Mom! It's Jesus!

Having Baby Jesus in our home means a lot to our family. He stayed on our entertainment center so all could see and remember that Jesus is in our lives everyday and is there for us whenever we need him. All we have to do is ask, and he will be there for us. Yesterday afternoon Baby Jesus stayed at Daddy's shop and watched him cut hair, and then he came home and enjoyed the rest of the night with our family.

In Christ's name,

Lindsay Langley

Denise Nutt-Beers

Lisa and Allen came to us from another United Methodist congregation. Lisa shared her talents with the children's and youth choirs, while Allen put his to work on beautiful storage cabinets for the Sunday School rooms. In very unique ways, Lisa and Allen leave beautiful footprints on the hearts of Spring Hill UMC.

Blessed be the Lord, who daily bears us up; God is our salvation.

Psalm 68:19

Hey Mom! It's Jesus!

This was our first time with Baby Jesus sharing our home. He came to us on a special night. It was our 9th wedding anniversary. Every day is a gift from God. This year there were times I forgot that. I look at Baby Jesus' eyes and out-reached arms and remember: those arms are reaching out to us. When we can't carry our burdens any longer, those arms will carry the load for us. His eyes cry the tears we can no longer shed. There is hope in Jesus. Precious babe, my love for you has no end and no bounds. I receive the gift of your presence in our home, hearts and lives. Let the light of your spirit illuminate the path before us. Let me never forget again you are part of me and your love is there every hour of every day. Thank you Jayne Leitze for letting me care for Baby Jesus.

Lisa and Allen Bean

Denise Nutt-Beers

Toby visits, sends cards and remembers in prayer every sick person in the church and community. She is instrumental in organizing prayer vigils, getting the word out for church events and keeping the gospel alive. I so admire her perseverance, as well as her unparalleled optimism.

Peace I leave with you; my peace I give to you. I do not give to you as the world gives. Do not let your hearts be troubled, and do not let them be afraid.

John 14:27

Hey Mom! It's Jesus!

Lisa's delivery visit was a pleasure – chatty and relaxing for us (sharing time).

Any small infant seems innocent but what a difference HIS lifetime made!

Appreciated the peaceful feeling of Baby Jesus.

Toby

Denise Nutt-Beers

Another entry from a child with a story that is almost an aside, yet one that is profound in its simple statement: Good things happen. Bad things happen. Jesus is there.

God is our refuge and strength, a very present help in trouble.

Psalm 46:1

Hey Mom! It's Jesus!

Receiving Baby Jesus was a big joy for our family. When we went home, I put Baby Jesus on my headboard and there he slept for the night. Saturday night at my basketball game my teammate, Rachel's, father had a seizure. They put him on the stretcher and left. They called the game, and I had remembered that Jesus was watching him. Now Baby Jesus is going to another house for a day.

Love,

Shana Edwards

Denise Nutt-Beers

Emily is in college now. I trust that the faith she knew as a child will under gird her as she strikes out on her own. I also pray that she remembers the words she wrote these many years ago, as she ventures out into a big, new world.

No one shall be able to stand against you all the days of your life. As I was with Moses, so I will be with you; I will not fail you or forsake you.

Joshua 1:5

Hey Mom! It's Jesus!

Having Baby Jesus in our home was a blessing. He stayed by my bed last night. Having Baby Jesus makes me remember that Jesus is with us all the time. He never leaves us. He takes care of us and watches over us all the time. Hopefully, everyone feels the same way.

Merry Christmas,

Emily Cathey

Denise Nutt-Beers

Susan and Joe are such sweet, gentle souls. Susan can often be seen in her trademark hat on any given Sunday. The Cathey's shared Baby Jesus with them at such a special time – the day they made the choice to have Spring Hill UMC be their permanent church family.

Always eager to offer an encouraging word or hug of support, Joe and Susan exhibit the tenderness and kindness of Jesus.

Do not neglect to show hospitality to strangers, for by doing that some have entertained angels without knowing it.

Hebrews 13:2

Hey Mom! It's Jesus!

Having Baby Jesus at our house is such a joy. Today we changed our church membership to Spring Hill, and tonight we received the honor of participating in this wonderful tradition. I think we've found a wonderful church family that has welcomed us and made us feel at home! There have been many changes in our lives over the last few months. Moving to a new community while our oldest son remains in East TN, and all the adjusting that goes along with a move had been made easier because of the friendliness we've encountered here.

Tonight looking at Baby Jesus I am reminded that we in fact "entertaining Jesus" each time we reach out to help another in his name. I can aspire to "entertain Jesus" in my heart and home each day. What a privilege that is!

Susan Kay

Denise Nutt-Beers

My children, playing a game with their friend Jesus... He couldn't really play, being a figurine and all, but that didn't bother them. What he could not do, they did for him. What other blessings do we need?

At that time Jesus said, "I thank you, Father, Lord of heaven and earth, because you have hidden these things from the wise and the intelligent and have revealed them to infants..."

Matthew 11:25

Hey Mom! It's Jesus!

Last night, quite unexpectedly, our doorbell rang. We answered it and found Jesus there! The newest members of the Spring Hill United Methodist family, Joe and Susan Kay, brought him to us. It was such an honor for them to remember us with the Christ Child. We were so pleased to receive them at Spring Hill along with their son, Jordan.

Our children always love to host the Baby Jesus. This morning the two little ones, Maylen and Jackson, were in the den playing Memory. As I listened to their chatter, I heard Maylen say, "Okay Jesus' turn! Pick one for him!" "Okay!" Jackson answered, and they proceeded to play.

Every day I am amazed at the ability of children to accept God and the things of God. To them having Jesus here is as normal as any other dear friend or family member.

Denise

When I was a young person, one of the most special times of my life was seeing "The Nativity Scene" in Centennial Park. It's not there anymore. The Baby Jesus in that scene, the Christmas music of old, not "Jingle Bell Rock" or "Grandma Got Run Over By A Reindeer", but the ancient of days music, the cool crisp air, close friends, and the emotional feelings of the moment.

When I see Baby Jesus now, even in the bustle of malls, parking lots and such, those feelings return. I hope everyone who had the opportunity to receive Baby Jesus somehow can receive the true meaning. Touching the small fingers, the tiny toes and realizing what this child has done for us. O come, Emmanuel.

Jim

Denise Nutt-Beers

James, Joan and their girls, Heather, Katie and Shelby remind all who meet them that Jesus is to be part of our everyday lives, not just someone in white robes to visit on Sundays at 11:00. As a nurse in a busy urban hospital, Joan ministers to people as they go to and from day surgery. A truck driver both locally and over-the-road, James encounters and uses many opportunities to share the story of Jesus.

James and Joan are raising three daughters and now a son in faith and love. Their commitment to their children can be seen in their little faces whenever one or the other of them enters the room. The Scruggs have much to teach us about taking Jesus from the pretty stained glass and out into the streets where there are hurts to be healed, wounds to be tended and souls to be saved.

If you then, who are evil, know how to give good gifts to your children, how much more will your Father in heaven give good things to those who ask him!

Matthew 7:11

Hey Mom! It's Jesus!

Baby Jesus was delivered to our door last night. It was such a pleasure to visit with Denise and to receive the Christ Child. He was placed on our entertainment center to be protected from the little one (Shelby) and so he could be seen by all. As I look at Baby Jesus, I think of how so many of us got caught up in the hectic pace of the "commercialized" Christmas, and we lose the true meaning of the season. As I am reminded of this, I can only hope I succeed in putting Christ back in Christmas. Heather told me having Baby Jesus in our house made her think of the true meaning of Christmas saying, "It's not about the gifts we receive, it's about the love."

Joan Scruggs

Denise Nutt-Beers

If nothing else, (and certainly there were many other things), hosting the Baby Jesus gave so many parents, including the Taylors, an extra motivation for discussing Jesus with their children.

When I think of you on my bed, and meditate on you in the watches of the night; for you have been my help, and in the shadow of your wings I sing for joy. My soul clings to you; your right hand upholds me.

Psalm 63: 6 - 8

Hey Mom! It's Jesus!

Thursday night was a very special night for the Taylor family. At about 6:00 p.m. we received the Baby Jesus. We were very pleased to have the Baby Jesus in our home again this year.

When we put our son, Zachary down for bed, we put the Baby Jesus on the dresser next to the bed. We told Zach how Jesus watches over everyone and that he would watch over him while he slept.

Having the Baby Jesus in our home reminds us what Christmas is all about. We hope that it does the same for others.

Thank you and Merry Christmas,

Danny and Beverly Taylor and Zachary

Denise Nutt-Beers

Epiphany! Christ is in Christmas! Oh, that it were always so.

...And that Christ may dwell in your hearts through faith, as you are being rooted and grounded in love.

Ephesians 3:17a

Hey Mom! It's Jesus!

We received "Baby Jesus" today at church from Ken And Bailey Loveless. Meredith and Hannah carefully placed him near our Christmas tree.

During the day, Meredith was working on her spelling words. She had spelled Christmas wrong by leaving out the "t". I asked her if she realized that the word "Christ" was in Christmas, and you could tell by her eyes lighting up, she didn't! At that time, I wondered how many of us really leave "Christ" out of Christmas.

By having Baby Jesus in our house again this year it has been a real blessing and brings us closer to the real meaning of Christmas.

Merry Christmas!

The Burgess Family

Denise Nutt-Beers

The Hughes were welcomed into the family of God, Spring Hill branch, with open arms. To look back and see what fruit a handshake or a kind word bears must be a powerful witness for those who reached out to this family in Christian love.

...*Go home to your friends, and tell them how much the Lord has done for you, and what mercy he has shown you.*

Mark 5:19

Hey Mom! It's Jesus!

We received Baby Jesus about 8:30 p.m. on Monday. What an honor to be a part of this tradition for the second year in a row. Last year we were not even members of the church, but were treated as part of the family. This year we are members of the church. The four of us were baptized and joined the church on Easter Sunday. Our family seems to grow each Sunday. It is so wonderful to be a part of this church and tradition.

We placed "Baby Jesus" in our living room, where we spent most of our family time together.

Thanks to the Burgess' family for remembering our family during this very special tradition.

Jimmy, Melissa, Whitney, and Jessica

Denise Nutt-Beers

Blessed with angelic voices and unparalleled commitment to God, Martha and Brittney freely offer their gifts and talents, not only to the church, but also to all that they do. Martha fills any need in the church whether it is sewing, preparing communion, song-leading, baking, teaching, cleaning or leading worship. A core member of the youth group, Brittney follows closely in her mother's footsteps. Many times, I would look around in need only to find Martha already there, quietly putting things back together.

Along with her Biblical namesake, Martha makes sure that people are fed, that things are in order and that needs are met. I would not have been the pastor I was without her constant support.

On that day you will ask in my name. I do not say to you that I will ask the Father on your behalf.

John 16:26

Hey Mom! It's Jesus!

Last night we had just returned from the E.A. Cox Christmas Band concert, when we got the call that the Baby Jesus was coming to our house. Brittney was so excited. This would be the first time we have had him come to our house. He sat at the table while she finished her homework, and she put him on her nightstand to sleep. I think she really wanted him to go to school with her today, but he came to work with me. Tonight he will go home with someone else. There will be a slight physical absence at out home but the spirit of Jesus and the true meaning of Christmas will remain there forever.

Merry Christmas to all,

Martha and Brittney

Denise Nutt-Beers

It may take a village to raise a child, but it takes the family of God to raise a Christian. Whatever the Leitze family received from the church, they gave back tenfold.

And he took them up in his arms, laid his hands on them, and blessed them.

Mark 10:16

Hey Mom! It's Jesus!

Once again we have been blessed with the gift of having Baby Jesus in our home. This gives us the opportunity to reflect on Jesus' presence in our lives over the past year. Throughout the saga of the Leitze-Garner family, he has been at our side. Actually, he has carried us many times in the past year. Much of the time there would have been only one set of footprints in the sand. It is through his unconditional love and support that we have survived with our sanity intact! Jesus led us to this church almost nine years ago. Our lives have been truly enriched. The people of this church truly are the embodiment of Christ. They have been there for us more times than we can count. There is a book, <u>It Takes a Village to Raise a Child</u>. This church has been our village. Everyone in it is such a part of who our children are, and the adults they are becoming. We are honored and proud to be a part of this Family of God. Thank you, Baby Jesus, for showing us the way.

Christian love to all,

Connie, Darrell, Travis, Jayna and Keisha Noel.

We feel so blessed that our "family" has grown so much this year! So many new members! Praise the Lord!

Denise Nutt-Beers

Jayna's last three sentences make the whole Baby Jesus tradition worthwhile. She is beautiful – inside and out. I pray that she will always remember the words she wrote here, all these years ago.

Do not worry about anything, but in everything by prayer and supplication with thanksgiving let your requests be made known to God.

Philippians 4:6

Hey Mom! It's Jesus!

My experiences with Baby Jesus have changed me over the years. This year I started praying 2 or 3 times a day. That has changed me a lot. Even though I pray in my head, he still hears me. I believe he is what gave me the courage to become a group leader in prayer group at school. He had blessed me with love for him, other people and myself. I used to not like myself because people tease me. They tease me about being overweight. If I hear someone teasing I am going to tell him or her, "I am happy with myself because God made me who I am."

Jayna Dawn Leitze

Denise Nutt-Beers

There is a saying in Christian communities that, if you have a praying grandmother, watch out! It may take a little while, but God always listens and God always answers! Jamie's grandmother prayed for over 11 years that Jamie would be saved and get baptized. And don't you know – her prayers were answered! Not only was Jamie baptized, but his whole household including his wife, Michelle, and daughters, Sarah and Rachel.

I have said these things to you so that my joy may be in you, and that your joy may be complete.

John 15:11

Hey Mom! It's Jesus!

The birth of Jesus marked a turning point for the world.

Having Baby Jesus in our home reinforced the commitment of the turning point in our lives.

This will be the first Christmas I have ever given any thought to the important side of it. The true meaning of this day and the spirituality that goes with it has added a new level of joy and peace to me.

Thanks to our "new family" for sharing this honor with us and for helping us find our way.

Merry Christmas to all,

Jamie, Michelle, Sarah and Rachel

Denise Nutt-Beers

Janie is one of the folks that people think of when they think "Jesus", so it is not surprising to me that even the newest of families would remember her. She shares Jesus with the multitudes each and every day.

May the God of hope fill you with all joy and peace in believing, so that you may abound in hope by the power of the Holy Spirit.

Romans 15:13

Hey Mom! It's Jesus!

On Dec. 15, Freddie and I were away attending a Christmas play that our granddaughter, Shelley, was participating in. We missed a call to host Baby Jesus. I was so disappointed, for I have had our church Baby Jesus for a while. But I thought it's ok, someone else may need him tonight. (I think God works that way!) For I was still very excited from the wonderful feelings that remained in my heart from that Children's Choir program and the beautiful cantata presented by the Adult Choir. This year had been joyous! My involvement with the Children's Choir ministry is a constant reminder of Christ working and living in our lives. If only I could look at life through their eyes and spirits, what a better person I would be! Then today (Dec. 19) I was busy preparing an evening meal for my family because my children, their spouses and our three precious grandchildren were coming over to celebrate our Christmas together, when the phone rang. Michelle asked if I would like to have Baby Jesus for the night. "Yes, how perfect," I told her for my family would be together tonight. How wonderful to be remembered by this lovely family that have recently entered my life, sharing their love for Christ and choosing our church as their new family. God has richly blessed us by sending many new families to SH choosing us to be their church family. For me this year has been filled with joy and hope. Even during my trials and temptations, I face each new day with the hope Jesus promises. I pray that I can share a piece of that faith and hope with others. Hosting Baby Jesus was an additional reminder of the many blessing God has given to my family and me.

Janie Murphy

Denise Nutt-Beers

Mary Lou's words are brief and concise. A strong and capable mother, she is indeed blessed with a wonderful son. While at times shy, he has a jovial sense of humor and a caring heart. He is, as we say down south, a "fine young man."

Hear, my child, your father's instruction, and do not reject your mother's teaching; for they are a fair garland for your head, and pendants for your neck.

Proverbs 1:8 - 9

Hey Mom! It's Jesus!

God has been good to me and my family, but most of all, I am blessed with a beautiful son.

Mary Lou

Denise Nutt-Beers

Inez's* family enjoys a long history at Spring Hill UMC. Her father donated the land on which the parsonage stood for over five decades. The land lay between her parents' and her sister's house on Main Street. Her mother kept close ties with each pastor as they came and went over time. She cared for an invalid daughter for years before breaking her hip and becoming housebound. She loved for the preacher to visit with her on the expansive front porch or in the back den of her house.

Every afternoon around 3:30 or so, Inez would walk the ½ mile trek from her house to her mother's to visit with her. Such devotion to one's parent is uncommon these days. But not in Inez's case. Even when she, herself, became ill with cancer, she still came to care for her mother, as did her other family members.

Inez a true survivor. She has faced each battle with great heartiness. Although she recently lost her husband after his years of battling emphysema, she continues to be a pillar of faith, setting high standards for herself, her church and her community.

**And be kind to one another, tender-hearted, forgiving one another,
as God in Christ has forgiven you.**

Ephesians 4:32

Hey Mom! It's Jesus!

Mary Lou chose to bring "Baby Jesus" to our house on a cold, windy afternoon. Even though the little carving is only a symbol, it brings the tremendous need for love and kindness to be felt and demonstrated throughout our lives, always, not just during the Christmas season.

Inez

Denise Nutt-Beers

"One look at Jesus" and Susan was back on track. What if the entire world could have such faith? As Christians we are taught to trust God in all things; yet we constantly forget. Susan's words are a gentle reminder that with God all things are possible.

Looking to Jesus the pioneer and perfecter of our faith, who for the sake of the joy that was set before him endured the cross, disregarding its shame, and has taken his seat at the right hand of the throne of God.

Hebrews 12:2

Hey Mom! It's Jesus!

Having Baby Jesus with us this day has been a blessing. When things got a little frustrating all I needed was one look at Baby Jesus to put me back on track to what was really important. We enjoy having the Baby Jesus in our house every year and look forward to his visits. I plan to purchase a Baby Jesus so he will remind us everyday what really is important.

God Bless and Merry Christmas.

Mark and Susan Dexter, Jessica and Joseph

With Jesus' amazing grace and forgiving love, one would never know he carried the wounds of his hands, feet and sides for the salvation of the very ones who put them there.

He restores my soul. He leads me in right paths for his name's sake.

Psalm 23:3

Hey Mom! It's Jesus!

It was a warm, rainy night. Everyone slept so well. You would have never known "Baby Jesus" had a broken hand; he was so quiet and "peaceful"! He helps remind us of what these holidays are really all about.

He guards, guides and directs us in the right ways. He's a very nice guest to have around.

Hope he helps us have a better year.

Love,

Joe and Emily

Denise Nutt-Beers

And it is in his wounds that we are healed...

The wind blows where it chooses, and you hear the sound of it, but you do not know where it comes from or where it goes. So it is with everyone who is born of the Spirit.

John 3:8

Hey Mom! It's Jesus!

Happy Holidays!

Now was a good time for us to receive the Baby Jesus. It's been a time for us to feel the love that he brings into our world.

We've had a lot going on in our families with our moms.

Dan's mom was having bad pains in her shoulder and thought she might have to have surgery before Christmas. They found out today that they could help her without surgery.

My mom was in the hospital last week even on Thanksgiving. Thank goodness she is doing better now but undergoes some tests tomorrow.

I know the Lord is always with us. I can feel his touch when the wind blows.

Having Baby Jesus helps warm our home, strengthen our faith and get us ready to handle the rough times as much as the smooth.

We were already in a Christmas mood. Now we're ready to celebrate the birth of the Lord.

Merry Christmas to all and we wish everyone a wonderful 1999.

"The Davidsons"

Dan, Sandy, Leslie and Terry

Denise Nutt-Beers

Children see beauty where we see brokenness and shame. Jesus "suffered" a broken hand somewhere along the way, which bothered many people and gave me a visual for some unique teaching. The children, however, were impervious. They proclaimed him beautiful "even though his hand is broken" and his "arm torn off"

To adults, however, a broken Jesus is still as disturbing to us as it was to the women who gathered at the cross on the first Good Friday. Mary, cradling her son at his birth, could not have imagined the wounds in his flesh at his death. For us, too, a broken Jesus is almost inconceivable. A wounded Savior? How could that be? Then again, how could it not be?

He himself bore our sins in his body on the cross, so that, free from sins, we might live for righteousness; by his wounds you have been healed. For you were going astray like sheep, but now you have returned to the shepherd and guardian of your souls.

1 Peter 2:24 - 25

Hey Mom! It's Jesus!

I have had the Baby Jesus in my class and home for three days now – I know that that is more than the recommended visit. I have hardly realized he is here. This reminds me that Jesus is always with us watching over us, even when we are so busy with everyday life that we forget he is there for a while. He doesn't forget us, ever. He is a constant force in our lives even when we don't realize it.

I was disturbed when he arrived to find his hand broken, especially when the person who delivered him did not mention that he was broken. After I read a few pages I realized that he had been broken for a while. I wanted to repair him but did not have the proper kind of glue. Perhaps someone he visits will be able to restore him to his whole state.

I realized then that he could return to us as a handicapped person. He could return to us as anyone in any state of health. That gave me a lot to think about. More of my children who wanted to write in the book did not have time. I think I will set up a center in my class where children can write about him coming to visit, if they like. Then I will send their comments to Denise to add to this book.

I am so grateful for this ministry of the visit of Jesus. It always brings me back down to earth, thinking about the real reason we celebrate Christmas. It also gives me a chance to share him with others who may not have a chance to know him otherwise.

Thank you.

Love,

Sue

Denise Nutt-Beers

Melissa faced a familiar circumstance as a single mother of two lovely dark-haired girls. Sweet and joyous babies, Taylor and Mackenzie reminded everyone of the wonder and beauty of God.

Keep your lives free from the love of money, and be content with what you have; for he has said, "I will never leave you or forsake you."

Hebrews 13:5b

Hey Mom! It's Jesus!

We are thrilled to have Baby Jesus in our home for a few days. It has been a wonderful opportunity to discuss with Taylor the true meaning of Christmas and why we celebrate. It had also been a great opportunity to examine my behavior and actions in my everyday life. We have brought Baby Jesus to stay with us for a few days, but in reality, Jesus is with us every minute of every day. This realization is comforting. We hope to have the honor each year of having our Baby Jesus come into our home and remind us of the things that are most important during the Christmas season.

Melissa

Denise Nutt-Beers

Stories of pregnancy and birth were not uncommon in Biblical days; nor are they uncommon in Jesus' modern journeys.

***Know that the Lord is God. It is he that made us, and we are his;
we are his people, and the sheep of his pasture.***

Psalm 100:3

Hey Mom! It's Jesus!

We were so honored to have Baby Jesus in our home. It was during this time with us that we found out that he had once again blessed our family with a new addition. He helps us remember that all things are from him. He fills our daily lives with hope for a better tomorrow.

Renee Martin

Denise Nutt-Beers

Bringing Jesus home from church may just be the newest radical movement. So many want to leave him at the door, pick him up 10 minutes before worship, sit with him through church, and then leave him at the door until the next week. Sue and Fred are not so inclined. They live and breathe Christ every day, not only at Christmas, but also throughout the year.

Every generous act of giving, with every perfect gift, is from above, coming down from the Father of lights, with whom there is no variation or shadow due to change.

James 1:17

Hey Mom! It's Jesus!

We brought Baby Jesus home with us from church 12 days before Christmas.

During his short stay, he was never far from us, which is the way it should always be.

Before we left to share him with others in our community, we placed him briefly under our Christmas tree.

Of all the things we give and receive, we must remember he is God's gift to us – and nothing is more important.

Denise was so right when she preached that there is much more to Christmas than the many frantic things we focus on.

Merry Christmas and a blessed New Year to all!

Love,

Fred and Sue

Denise Nutt-Beers

As the grandchildren began to come along, Sam and Frances began to slow down and refocus their lives. With a new generation comes a new opportunity to teach the love of Jesus. As do their children, I am sure that their grandchildren will remember Frances and Sam as strong in their faith, full in their love and incredible in their strength.

As God's chosen ones, holy and beloved, clothe yourselves with compassion, kindness, humility, meekness, and patience.

Colossians 3:12

Hey Mom! It's Jesus!

Once again we are blessed with having the tiny Baby Jesus with us in our homes for Christmas – this beautiful bundle of joy and hope who is so dependent on us to get him safely from home to home while we are still so totally dependent on him to get us through our day-to-day activities. He is once again my reminder of what Christmas is all about, and helps me bring the frantic rush of preparation for the material aspects of Christmas back into a more proper perspective.

Thank you. Although you are physically moving on to visit others, you remain in our hearts, always.

Peace and love to all.

Sam and Frances Smith

Denise Nutt-Beers

Surviving her first years as a widow, Mrs. Quirk still offers blessings and love to all who know her. What a gentle and genteel lady!

You show me the path of life. In your presence there is fullness of joy;
in your right hand are pleasures for evermore.

Psalm 16:11

Hey Mom! It's Jesus!

It is a wonderful blessing we enjoy all the year round to experience the loving care we enjoy when we have the presence of Jesus in our home and our life, day to day.

We pray that everyone will have this great gift that God has given us.

Elma Lee Quirk

Denise Nutt-Beers

Leroy faced many difficult months as he and Gloria wrote this last entry in the journal on this, the last journey of the Baby Jesus. Days of uncertainty, pain, sickness and risk would fill the next year of his life. However, days of hope and well-being would undergird him as well. The good news is that we now know the rest of the story. Leroy survived his cancer and his treatments. He is whole and well today. God is so good.

Do not let your hearts be troubled. Believe in God, believe also in me.

John 14:1

Hey Mom! It's Jesus!

Our family is really appreciative of having Baby Jesus visit us this weekend. It reminds us that he, too, came as a baby to earth to live and teach mankind what God, his and our heavenly father, wants us to do in our lives.

Jesus is always our safe haven from the "storms of life". He comforts us and helps us through the wonderful times and the sad, hurting times.

I notice that Jesus' arm and hand are now repaired. Someone repaired his hand and arm just he way he can mend our hearts, minds and bodies.

Leroy has battled lymphoma cancer this year and is checking out real well now. He had commented that he could feel all the prayers of so many people during this terrible illness. He feels that Jesus and God cared for him during this and made him well.

Leroy is to begin a new treatment on Dec. 29 that is going to help keep the cancer from coming back. He is trusting in Jesus and God to carry him through this new Treatment, and we all pray that it will do what is had been developed to do.

Leroy and our whole family are thankful that Jesus came to save us all and to make a place for us in his kingdom.

As we send Baby Jesus to another home, may he bless that home and all the other homes and families in the world.

Leroy and Gloria Burns

Denise Nutt-Beers

*Someone "fixed" the little Baby Jesus. He was broken
– for us. He is now whole – for us. And so, where in
the world is the little Baby Jesus?
Let every heart prepare him room!
Sweet little Jesus Boy.
He lives
within
our hearts!*

Appendix

Starting a "Baby Jesus" Ministry in Your Faith Community

1. Obtain a small Baby Jesus figurine such as the kind you might find in a table-top manger scene. When I started the ministry, I purchased a figurine for each congregation. One year, I misplaced one of them. After frantic searching, I remembered that I had at least 10 separate Jesus figurines in my own manger scenes. Sending one of them out "into the world" was a risk, to be sure. But isn't sharing Jesus always risky? Without hesitation, I sent the Baby Jesus from the manger scene my mother brought me from the Holy Land into the community that Advent. In the years since, that little wooden Christ Child is the most precious of all that I own...not because he came from the Holy Land, but because he journeyed through the homes of Spring Hill, Tennessee. Perhaps you or someone in your church would like to share a baby with the community.
2. Obtain a journal to accompany Jesus on his journey. A simple spiral notebook is fine.
3. Place the instructions in the front of the journal so that everyone understands the ministry and its intent. These should include:
    - You have been chosen to be part of the Baby Jesus Ministry of XYZ Church.

- Please keep Jesus for 24 hours.
- Record your experiences in the journal provided. What was it like to have Jesus in your household? Let children write their own entries!
- Please sign the front of the journal so that those who come after you can see the homes where Jesus has been.
- Please call the pastor or leader to make let him/her know you have Jesus when you receive him.
- By 6:00 p.m. the next day, take Jesus to another family or household. Let the Lord guide your choice.
- Remember the shut-ins or those in nursing facilities. Offer to bring Jesus to them and then to retrieve him and take him to another family for them.
- Jesus does not necessarily need to remain only among the member of the faith community. Perhaps a neighbor or a seeker needs him for the night. Again, let the Lord guide you.
- If you have Jesus on Christmas Eve (or other ending time if you do not have services on this day), please bring him to the celebration of his birth. If you cannot be at the service, please call the pastor or leader to make arrangements for Jesus to be picked up.

Hey Mom! It's Jesus!

4. Choose a household to host the baby Jesus for the first Sunday night in Advent. There are no rules…perhaps someone who has had particular struggles throughout the year or a new person in the congregation. Each family who hosts the baby will choose the next family. There is no list prepared ahead of time.
5. During the first Sunday in Advent, carefully explain the ministry to the congregation. Include an explanation in the bulletin if you use one.
6. Send Jesus out into the community.
7. Include mention of the ministry each Sunday during Advent. Let folks briefly share experiences with the congregation. I found it interesting that Jesus was only brought to church about half the time!
8. At the Christmas Eve or other service that marks the end of the ministry, share journal entries as the sermon or lesson.
9. If your congregation is very large, Sunday School classes, choirs or other groups can have individual Baby Jesus ministries. Resist the urge to buy a lot of figurines to make sure everybody is included. Part of the mystery and mystique of the ministry is the journey of Jesus within a community. The ministry is not about inclusion as much at it is about the miracles and the epiphanies Jesus brings.
10. Finally, be creative! Perhaps your congregation would like to purchase a figurine to send out into the world at large, without expecting him to "return". Contact information for the church could be in the journal, just in case. Ideas for sharing

Jesus are as numerous as there are Christians. May the Baby Jesus Ministry bless you and the world.